THE POWER OF
THE 4TH WATCH

THE POWER OF THE 4TH WATCH

Dr. C.A. Turner

J. Kenkade
PUBLISHING®
LITTLE ROCK, ARKANSAS

The Power of the 4th Watch
Copyright © 2021 Carlos Turner

Printed in the United States of America

J. Kenkade Publishing
6104 Forbing Rd
Little Rock, AR 72209
www.jkenkadepublishing.com
Facebook.com/jkenkadepublishing

J. Kenkade Publishing is a registered trademark.

Printed in the United States of America
ISBN 978-1-955186-11-7

Unless otherwise noted, scripture quotations are taken from the King James Version® Bible, Public Domain. Used by permission. All rights reserved.

The views expressed in this book are those of the author and do not necessarily reflect the views of Publisher.

Table of Contents

Introduction

Being a front-line warrior is not easy at times! There is a price to pay with your life, and it takes much sacrifice and commitment to the purpose and plans of God. Watching is an assignment that will cost you something, but with obedience comes blessings, miracles and spiritual assistance from heaven! I'm sure you have read my book *Supernatural Invasion*, but allow me to refresh your spirit with some notes you need to know moving forward.

When you are watching you are fasting, praying, and abstaining from sleep for certain periods of time. You become an ***Intercessor***! An individual that can stand in the gap for someone else while they are asleep! They enter in and out of different realms, dimensions, and spheres of the spirit without titles and validation!!!

So let's find out what a Watch is.

The word "Watch" comes from the Greek word **(KOU'STODIA)**, which we get our English word *"Custody"* from. It means to manage, to take custody and control of. Which means you must be spiritually alert, awaken, and ready to exercise spiritual authority when necessary!

What will a WATCH do????

1. It will Strengthen your anointing of discernment
2. It will Make you Spiritually Sensitive
3. It will Give you Spiritual Awareness
4. It will Uncover the intentions & assignments of the devil
5. It will Give you uncommon grace and Wisdom

The 4 WATCHES of the night is in three-hour shifts! You have the first watch, and second watch and the third watch and the one we are going to be discussing in this book is the fourth watch! Let's take a look at them.

1st – (6pm-9pm)
2nd – (9pm – 12am)
3rd – (12am – 3am)
4th – (3am – 6am)

It's very imperative that you know that each Watch has its own POWER and anointing! When you are lead of the spirit the father gives you supernatural high definition discernment and knowledge about things that's happening, and things to come so that you can warn the people before it happens. Let's take a look in the word.

Again the word of the LORD came unto me, saying, Son of man, speak to the children of thy people, and say unto them, When I bring the sword upon a land, if the people of the land take a man of their coasts, and set him for their watchman: If when he seeth the sword come upon the land, he blow the trumpet, and warn the people; Then whosoever heareth the sound of the trumpet, and taketh not warning; if the sword come, and take him away, his blood shall be upon his own head. He heard the sound of the trumpet, and took not warning; his blood shall be upon him. But he that taketh warning shall deliver his soul. But if the watchman see the sword come, and blow not the trumpet, and the people be not warned; if the sword come, and take any person from among them, he is taken away in his iniquity; but his blood will I require at the watchman's hand. So thou, O

son of man, I have set thee a watchman unto the house of Israel; therefore thou shalt hear the word at my mouth, and warn them from me.
Ezekiel 33:1-7

As you can see being a watchman is serious business! There's no room for error! You must be focused and obedient! Why is that important? Because watching can save a whole city from destruction and disaster! Are you ready?

RHEMA NOTES

_____

_____

_____

_____

_____

_____

_____

_____

_____

_____

_____

_____

_____

_____

_____

_____

_____

_____

_____

_____

_____

_____

_____

_____

_____

_____

_____

_____

_____

_____

_____

_____

_____

_____

_____

_____

_____

_____

_____

_____

_____

_____

_____

_____

Carlos Turner

✝

<u>The Power of the 4th Watch</u>

The fourth watch is the most powerful watch of them all! Have you ever been sleeping really good, and all of a sudden God starts waking you up at three or four o'clock in the morning? Instead of you getting up and praying, you go to the bathroom, and from the bathroom to the kitchen, and from the kitchen back to the bed. I know I'm in your business, however can you relate? Allow me to inform you, He didn't wake you up for a bowl of cereal, a sandwich, or a glass of water. That was a watchman wakeup call! You never know why he is waking you up, so it's always important to stay up and pray immediately!

The Jews see the fourth Watch as their **"Secret Place,"** and believe that God visits the earth 2 hours right before sunrise with favor to establish his Protection, Provision, Power, Prosperity and with his *Presence on behalf of his people!*

The fourth watch is the peak time for spiritual things and spiritual connections! Matter of fact, witches and warlocks meditate at this time of the night to get instructions from the kingdom of darkness! Those that work with the kingdom of darkness understand that this time is peak time, and that most Christians are in their bed asleep while the enemy is setting up traps and plots to ruin their day! But we are getting back in position to taking authority and advantage of the fourth watch! Come on! Let's take it back!

There's seven things you need to know at this Time:

1. This Watch is when angelic activity is at an all-time high.

2. A man words are at its strongest capacity, they become Spermatic.

3. Visions and Dreams are the clearest at this time.

4. Angelic Visitations are normal at this time.

5. Physical Demonic attacks are likely if

one is not covered.

6. It allows a believer to reconnect to spiritual power to destroy plots, plans and assignments of the enemy.

7. Decreeing, declaring and directing are your tools of power in this
Watch!

Supernatural things happen in the fourth watch! Even Jesus' disciples understood this! Jesus was coming to his disciples while walking on water, and they thought it was just a spirit or an angel. Why? Because it was common to see spirits and angels at this time even though they were afraid. Let's look in the word.

And when he had sent the multitudes away, he went up into a mountain apart to pray: and when the evening was come, he was there alone. But the ship was now in the midst of the sea, tossed with waves: for the wind was contrary. And in the fourth watch of the night Jesus went unto them, walking on the sea. And when the disciples saw him walking on the sea, they were troubled, saying, It is a spirit; and they cried out for fear. But straightway Jesus spake unto them, saying, Be of good cheer; it is I; be not afraid. And Peter answered him and said, Lord, if it be thou, bid me come unto thee on the water.And he said, Come. And when Peter was come down out of the ship, he walked on the water, to go to Jesus. But when he saw the wind boisterous, he was afraid; and beginning to sink, he cried, saying, Lord, save me. And immediately Jesus stretched forth his hand, and caught him, and said unto him, O thou of little faith, wherefore didst thou doubt?

And when they were come into the ship, the wind ceased.

Matthew 14:23–32

As you can see there were many supernatural things that took place in the fourth watch! It's so imperative that we have the spirit of Peter and say, "if it be you, bid me to come!" The father is waiting for somebody that's willing to step out the boat, out of their comfort zone and say "Lord it's me, I'm ready to step out and do what nobody beside you has ever done! Glory be to the lamb of God!"

Spending time with the Father in prayer in the fourth watch is you stepping out of the boat, preparing yourself to do supernatural things!

Are you an intercessor? This Watch is tailor-made just for you! Let's talk about your assignment in this hour.

An Intercessor is an individual that can stand in the gap for someone else! They enter in and out of different realms, dimensions and spheres of the spirit without titles and validation!!!

Now this watch is for 1st Sphere IN-TERCESSORS!!! Why? Because they are trailblazers in the spirit!!! It is important to also understand that experienced Intercessors know how to **CLOSE** the day out and **START** a day up with POWER!!!!

What are the desires of Intercessors? They have four desires:

1. See total Deliverance take place.
2. See Spiritual, Mental, Physical and Financial Freedom in the Body of Christ.
3. See a total recovery from a complete fall.
4. See Miracles, Signs and Wonders that lead to salvation.

If you are an Intercessor, you are either a Spiritual Watchman or a Spiritual Gatekeeper.

Please allow me to explain the different assignments and characteristics.

The Characteristic and assignment of a Spiritual Watchmen:

They work secretly behind the scenes
They want no ATTENTION at all
They are Not easily distracted but redirect distractions
They can sense the enemy and his attacks

The Characteristic and assignment of a Spiritual Gatekeeper:

They control the flow or the traffic of a place portal (Naturally and Spiritually)
They discern who is really with us and for us
They operate as spiritual Security
They are responsible for who and what penetrate the atmosphere

As you can see both can function in the watch but have different assignments! Now if a couple is married, the proper order for the marital (husband/wife) team is the husband is the Spiritual watchman and the Wife is the spiritual gatekeeper.

There are four things that I believe that's important to understand about Intercession.

1. Intercession can STOP death-
Gen 37:21-22, 26-27
2. Intercession can STOP hunger-
Jer 38:7-13
3. Intercession will reveal a gift and grant favor- **Gen 41:9-13, 40:14**
4. Intercession on the behalf of her son's future- **I King 1:15-31**

Intercession is a powerful spiritual tool to get things done in the earth. Let's take advantage of the power of the fourth watch and shift atmospheres and take back territory in Jesus' name!

Rhema Notes

_____

_____

_____

_____

_____

_____

_____

_____

_____

_____

_____

_____

_____

_____

_____

_____

_____

_____

_____

_____

_____

_____

_____

_____

_____

_____

_____

_____
_____
_____
_____
_____
_____
_____
_____
_____
_____
_____
_____
_____
_____
_____
_____
_____
_____
_____
_____
_____
_____
_____
_____
_____
_____
_____
_____

✝

The Conclusion of the Matter

As we delve more and more into the things of the spirit, we are going to discover new tools, tips, and strategies to equip us for the days to come. The enemy's job is to steal, kill, and to destroy, however we can't be ignorant of his devices. As we get closer to Jesus' return, you're going to notice that it's in the fourth watch where we receive power and insight! This is the time where we command our day and get ahead of the enemy! Spend time with God, don't allow no devil in hell to stop you from getting everything you need from God!

As we continue to seek the will of the Father, may His hands be upon you and may He guide you into all truth! I bless you my brothers and Sisters! May the Lord bless thee, may the Lord keep thee, the Lord make His face shine upon thee and be gracious to thee, may the Lord lift up His countenance upon thee and give thee peace! Shalom and Amen!

Rhema Notes

_____

_____

_____

_____

_____

_____

_____

_____

_____

_____

_____

_____

_____

_____

_____

_____

_____

_____

_____

_____

_____

_____

_____

_____

_____

_____

_____

_____

_____

_____

_____

_____

_____

_____

_____

_____

_____

_____

_____

_____

_____

_____

_____

_____

_____

_____

_____

_____

ABOUT THE AUTHOR

APOSTLE C. A. TURNER is the prophetic voice for this last hour. He is the Senior Pastor and Founder of Kingdom Nation Ministries and About God's Business World Outreach ministries in Jonesboro, AR and Memphis, TN. He has been preaching and teaching for over 25 years, reaching the lost at all cost and impacting the earth with the things concerning the kingdom of God with miracles, signs, and wonders operating within his ministry. He attended Grambling State University with a focus in Business Administration. He also Attended the School of Exodus studying Theology and Biblical Studies. He is the founder of Y.E.S.S. Young Entrepreneur Success School for the urban youth with a focus in financial Literacy. Carlos Turner is the owner and CEO of several successful businesses, Kingdom Clean Detailing, Tojoe's Wings and Waffles, Turner and Thomas Real Estate, Carlo Avery Fashions, and Olive Tree Finance and Investment Firm. In his spare time, he loves reading, studying, and researching the things of the spirit to stay sharp and alert for the things to come! His favorite verse is found in the book of Luke 1:37 that says, "For with God nothing shall be impossible!" His assignment is to shake and reawaken the body of Christ in the area of the supernatural. He understands that this will be a life journey, so he is totally committed to the things of God and strictly being about God's Business.

J. Kenkade
PUBLISHING®

Our Motto
"Transforming Life Stories"

Also Available from this Author

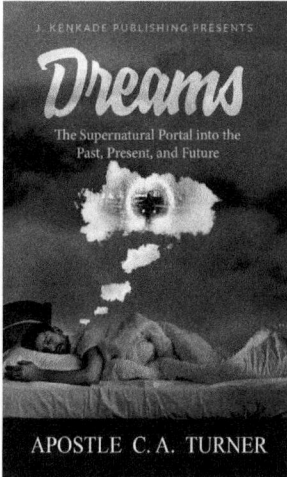

J. KENKADE PUBLISHING PRESENTS

Dreams
The Supernatural Portal into the
Past, Present, and Future

APOSTLE C. A. TURNER

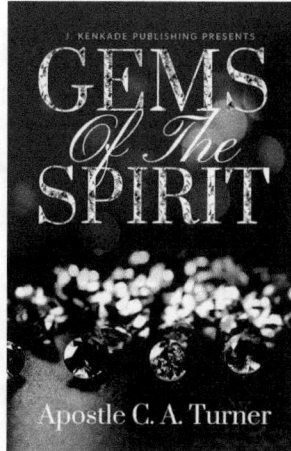

J. KENKADE PUBLISHING PRESENTS

GEMS
Of The
SPIRIT

Apostle C. A. Turner

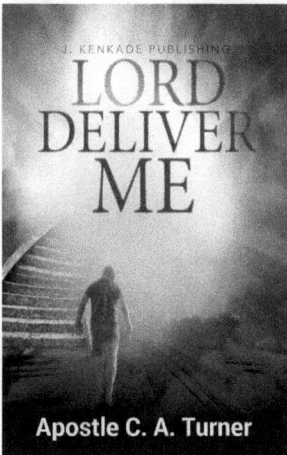

J. KENKADE PUBLISHING

LORD
DELIVER
ME

Apostle C. A. Turner

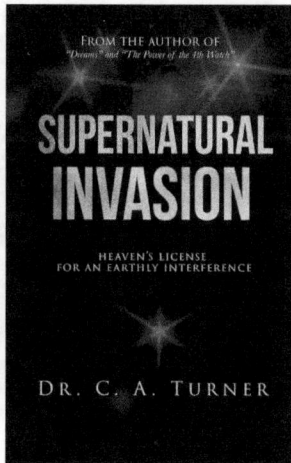

FROM THE AUTHOR OF
"Dreams" and "The Power of the 4th Watch"

SUPERNATURAL
INVASION

HEAVEN'S LICENSE
FOR AN EARTHLY INTERFERENCE

DR. C. A. TURNER

www.ingramcontent.com/pod-product-compliance
Lightning Source LLC
LaVergne TN
LVHW051207080426
835508LV00021B/2856